MY LIFE AS A

JEW WITHDRAWN

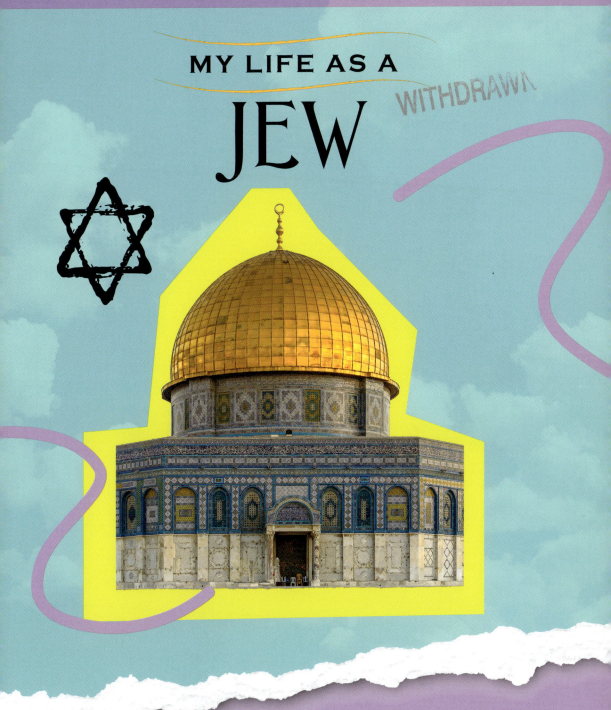

FLEUR BRADLEY

45th PARALLEL PRESS

Published in the United States of America by Cherry Lake Publishing Group
Ann Arbor, Michigan
www.cherrylakepublishing.com

Editorial Consultant: Dr. Virginia Loh-Hagan, EdD, Literacy, San Diego State University
Content Adviser: Molly H. Bassett, Associate Professor and Chair in the Department of Religious Studies
   at Georgia State University
Reading Adviser: Beth Walker Gambro, MS, Ed., Reading Consultant, Yorkville, IL
Book Designer: Jen Wahi

Photo Credits: © BargotiPhotography/istock, cover, 1; © Petr Pohudka/Shutterstock, 4; © yhelfman/Shutterstock, 8;
   © LaraP_photo/Shutterstock, 10; © Mike A. Martin/Shutterstock, 13; © David Cohen 156/Shutterstock, 14;
   © icon0.com/Shutterstock, 16; © Steve Boice/Shutterstock, 17; © TalyaAL/Shutterstock, 19; © Sopotnicki/
   Shutterstock, 20; © Donna Ellen Coleman/Shutterstock, 24; © Jim West/Alamy Stock Photo, 28; © Ilya
   Zuskovich/Shutterstock, 29; © Rachel K H/Shutterstock, 30

45th Parallel Press is an imprint of Cherry Lake Publishing Group.

Library of Congress Cataloging-in-Publication Data

Names: Bradley, Fleur, author.
Title: My life as a Jew / by Fleur Bradley.
Description: Ann Arbor, MI : Cherry Lake Publishing, 2022. | Series: How the world worships
Identifiers: LCCN 2021039843 | ISBN 9781534199439 (hardcover) | ISBN 9781668900574 (paperback) |
   ISBN 9781668906330 (ebook) | ISBN 9781668902011 (pdf)
Subjects: LCSH: Judaism—Juvenile literature. | Judaism—Essence, genius, nature—Juvenile literature.
Classification: LCC BM45 .B68 2022 | DDC 296—dc23
LC record available at https://lccn.loc.gov/2021039843

Printed in the United States of America
Corporate Graphics

ABOUT THE AUTHOR:

Fleur Bradley is originally from the Netherlands. She likes to travel and learn about different cultures whenever she can. Fleur has written many stories for kids and educational books. She now lives in Colorado with her family.

TABLE OF CONTENTS

Did you know? The Jewish Bible is called the Tanakh (tah-NAK). It consists of 3 books: the Torah, the Nevi'im (neh-vee-EEM), and the Ketuvim (kuh-too-VEEM). These books are the same books as the Old Testament in the Christian Bible. But they are in a different order.

Introduction

Religions are systems of faith and worship. Do you practice a religion? About 80 percent of the world's population does. That's 4 out of 5 people.

Every religion is different. Some have one God. That's called **monotheism**. Other religions have multiple gods. This is called **polytheism**. Some religions have an **icon** instead of a god. An icon is an important figure. Judaism is a monotheistic religion.

Judaism is the world's fifth largest religion. About 1 percent of the world's population is Jewish. In the United States, just under 2 percent of people consider themselves Jewish. Roughly 41 percent of Jews live in the Middle East and Africa.

Jewish people believe in one God. The sacred story of Judaism begins with Abraham. Sacred means holy. The story is told in the Torah. Abraham was a shepherd and married to Sarah. Almost 4,000 years ago, they lived in Ur, which is now Iraq. At the time, the people there believed in multiple gods.

Abraham wondered if one of these gods was the true god. God spoke to Abraham. He promised to bless Abraham and Sarah. God led them to Canaan. Canaan today is divided between Israel, Jordan, Lebanon, and Syria. God said Abraham would be the leader of the people. These people are called Hebrews. Abraham promised to be faithful to God.

A **famine** forced the Jews to leave Canaan. Famine means food shortage. They moved to Egypt. But as the Jewish population grew, Egyptians forced Jews into slavery.

God spoke to an Israelite called Moses. God told Moses that he needed to lead the people back to Canaan, the Promised Land.

THE HOLOCAUST

The Nazis were a political party in Germany from 1933 to 1945. They started World War II. They had power over most of Europe. The Nazis built concentration camps. Concentration camps are like prisons. But they are for people who didn't do anything wrong. The Nazis used these camps to torture and kill Jewish people. This terrible event in history is called the Holocaust.

At first, Jews in Europe were robbed of simple rights. They couldn't go to school. They couldn't go outside. Then they were forced to move to concentration camps.

Many Jews fought back. Many went into hiding. Some fled to other countries.

About 6 million Jews died in the Holocaust. That's about two-thirds of Europe's Jewish population.

Today people hold ceremonies to remember the Holocaust. They want to be sure that its horrors are never repeated.

Did you know? All Jewish temples have an Ark. It is also called the Ark of the Covenant. Covenant means promise. The sacred Torah is kept in the Ark.

Plagues followed and cursed the Egyptians. Plagues are diseases that spread quickly. Moses and the Jews roamed the desert for 40 years. This was when God gave Moses the 10 Commandments. These rules tell Jews how to live every day.

Today, there are 3 main branches of Judaism.

Orthodox Judaism believes you should strictly follow the rules God gave to Moses. Women and men usually sit separately during prayer. Men have a larger role in ceremonies. Orthodox Jews often wear black clothing.

Reform Judaism focuses on the ethics and values of their religion. Ethics are rules about what is good and bad. Reform Jews believe you don't have to exactly follow the religious text.

Conservative Judaism falls somewhere between Orthodox and Reform Judaism. Conservative Jews believe there can be change to religious practice. But this change should happen gradually.

Throughout history, conflict has followed the Jewish people. It caused them to disperse throughout the world. This is called **diaspora**.

In 1948, Israel was created as an independent state and Jewish homeland. This still causes conflict with the neighboring Arab state of Palestine.

Today, about 6.3 million people live in Israel. Just slightly less than 80 percent are Jewish.

Is there a Jewish temple in your area? What activities and celebrations are held there?

Ben
American Jew

CHAPTER 1
AN AMERICAN JEW

"Mr. Jones asked what it means to be Jewish," I say in front of my eighth-grade class. Today, we're discussing Judaism. "For me, it often means being different. I used to not like it," I add. "But now I'm proud to be Jewish."

I go on, "We pray every Friday to Saturday. We start on Friday at sundown. We end on Saturday at sundown. This is called **Shabbat**, or sabbath. It is a time of rest."

For my presentation, I took a photo that I show on the projector. "This is our **synagogue**. That's like a church, or a temple."

My classmate Ethan calls out, "I've seen that building in our neighborhood! I was wondering what it was."

Mr. Jones says, "Let's listen to Ben, so he can explain."

I show my next slide. "This is our **rabbi**. A rabbi is a teacher. He leads the Shabbat service every Friday evening and Saturday morning."

"So that's when you go to synagogue? You go on Saturday not on Sunday?" Sarah asks. Sarah's Catholic. She explained her faith last week.

"Exactly," I say. "Shabbat is the time for prayer and reflection. When we get to the synagogue, people greet us. They say *Shabbat shalom*. That means, 'Have a peaceful Shabbat.'"

"The rabbi then reads from the Torah," I add. "It's in Hebrew. Hebrew is the ancient language of Judaism."

"Do you know Hebrew?" Mr. Jones asks.

I nod. "I learned when I was young."

"Our holidays are different too," I say. I move to my next slide. "This candlestick is called a menorah. We light it for Hanukkah.

Ben talks about Hanukkah and its traditions. Can you find similarities to your own December holiday customs? What is different?

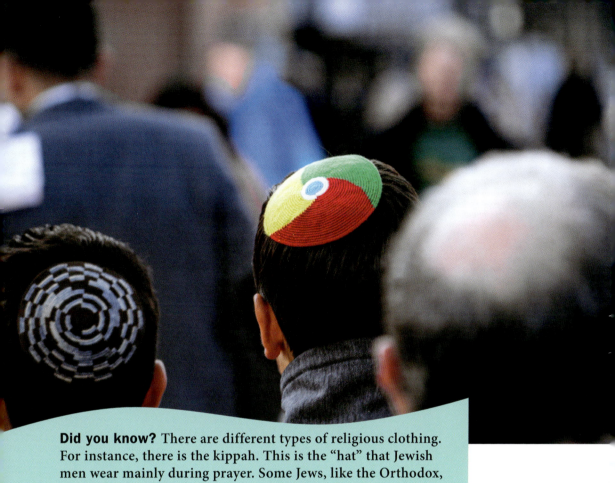

Did you know? There are different types of religious clothing. For instance, there is the kippah. This is the "hat" that Jewish men wear mainly during prayer. Some Jews, like the Orthodox, wear it at all times. It can have any design.

Hanukkah is also called the Festival of Lights. It celebrates the victory of the Maccabees over the Syrian Greek army. It also celebrates a miracle that happened. A candle meant to burn for only 1 day, ended up burning for 8 days! This is why Hanukkah is celebrated for 8 days."

"You don't celebrate Christmas, right?" Ethan asks.

"No," I smile. "But I do get presents for Hanukkah!"

Did you know? There are many ways to spell *Hanukkah.* There is *Hannuka, Chanukah,* and even *Xanuka*! This is because it had to first be transliterated from Hebrew to English. Transliterate means to spell a word from one alphabet to another.

CHAPTER 2
HANUKKAH IN THE UNITED STATES

The presentation at school went well. But I'm kind of glad it's done now.

I walk home with my younger sisters, relieved and ready for the second night of Hanukkah.

"Do you think we'll get those dolls we asked for?" my sister Rebekah whispers to Ruth. They're 7 and 9 years old. The presents are what they're excited about.

I look at Hanukkah differently. We went to Israel to visit our grandparents. There, almost everyone is Jewish! They don't exchange presents for Hanukkah. They celebrate with festivals instead.

At home, we help Mom and Dad make traditional foods for Hanukkah. Unlike my friend Sam's house, our kitchen is **kosher**. Kosher means permitted food for Jews. For example, dairy and meat are kept separate. Pork and shellfish are forbidden.

During World War II, Nazis made Jews wear a Star of David on their clothing. Today, some Jews wear the Star of David with pride. Can you think of why?

My dad is making **latkes**, my favorite. Latkes are delicious potato pancakes.

I sneak in a bite.

"Not until dinner, Benjamin!" Dad playfully scolds. He takes a bite too and gives me a smile. "These are excellent."

That evening, we play card games and sing songs. Our parents give us gelt, which are chocolate coins wrapped in foil.

My sisters get the dolls they want. I get a book. Then, we light the candle.

As we pray, I feel lifted by my faith. It's nice to be here with my family. I feel good about celebrating our faith.

We eat, and I tell my family about my presentation at school.

Did you know? The dreidel is a spinning top and game. Children often play this during Hanukkah. But it's not just for children. Dreidel spinning has gotten so popular that it's now a competitive sport in New York City!

HOLIDAYS

Here are some Jewish holidays that might be observed:

Passover: Celebrated in March or April, this holiday remembers God helping Moses guide the Israelites out of Egypt.

Rosh Hashanah: Celebration in September or October of the Jewish New Year and the creation of Adam and Eve.

Yom Kippur: Celebrated in September or October; calls on Jews to pray for forgiveness of their sins.

Hanukkah: Celebrated in early winter; remembers the story of Judas Maccabeus, a Jewish priest, who led the uprising against the Seleucid Empire.

Did you know? Most foods served during Hanukkah are fried. It acts as a reminder of the miracle. The miracle was when the oil meant for 1 day burned for 8.

"I'd be terrified!" Ruth says. She eats her *sufganiyot*, a jelly donut.

"It was okay," I said. "We've been talking about different religions in class. It's nice to learn more and share our history and traditions."

My dad smiles. "Like latkes," he says as he passes me the bowl.

I smile too. "These *are* the best."

Hannah
Israeli Jew

CHAPTER 3
A YOUNG JEW IN ISRAEL

My mother knocks on my bedroom door. "Are you ready, Hannah?" Today is a special day for me. It's my **bat mitzvah**.

Bat mitzvah means I become what's called the daughter of the Law. Boys go through the same ritual. But instead of a bat mitzvah, it's called a **bar mitzvah**. For Jewish girls and boys, it means you are an adult. This ritual happens when we turn 12 years old.

I'm already dressed for the day. I wear a long dress with long sleeves. My mom is also dressed nicely. It's an important celebration.

Our family goes to the synagogue together. I'm pretty nervous. We have a big congregation. That's all the people in our synagogue.

All of our family is here. I have a lot! Aunts, uncles, grandparents, and cousins all live near us. I'm pretty lucky.

THE 10 COMMANDMENTS

The 10 Commandments are part of the Jewish sacred text. They are said to be carved in stone tablets. These Commandments are rules all Jews should live by.

1. Love God more than anything else.

2. Don't make anything in life more important than God.

3. Say God's name with love and respect.

4. Honor the Lord by resting on Saturday.

5. Love and respect your mother and father.

6. Do not kill.

7. Respect marriage promises.

8. Do not steal.

9. Tell the truth.

10. Do not be jealous of what others have.

"Are you ready, Hannah?" my cousin Amir asks me. We're about the same age. He's having his bar mitzvah next year.

I nod. Before I can talk more, my mother takes me inside the synagogue. We meet our rabbi. Then I sit with my family until I get called up. That's called **aliyah**. Aliyah is the act of going to the reading table to read from the Torah.

Bat mitzvah ceremonies happen before the actual service. I read from the section of **Haftarah**. That's a portion of the Torah, our religious text.

I'm so nervous to read in front of everyone. But I only stumble over my words twice.

After I read, the rabbi leads the normal service. I sit with my family. I do my best to focus on the rabbi's words.

After the service, I'm showered with candy. That is to honor how sweet the moment of my bat mitzvah is.

My little cousins are allowed to pick up the candy. I don't mind, because there's a party ahead!

Hannah's bat mitzvah is a rite of passage for Jews. Can you think of other examples of this kind of ceremony?

CHAPTER 4
A BAT MITZVAH CELEBRATION

Finally, it's the party! We're having it at my grandparents' house, since there's more room. All my family is there.

We eat lots of great food. This meal after the bat mitzvah ceremony is called **s'udat mitzvah**. There are vegetables, boiled eggs, latkes, and lentil soup.

"I'm proud of you, Hannah," my grandmother says over dinner. "One of my friends mentioned how impressed she was by your mitzvah project."

A mitzvah project is something you do to help people. It's part of the preparation for your bar or bat mitzvah. I volunteered at the soup kitchen.

"Thank you, Grandma." I say. "Honestly, it was a lot of fun."
I like helping people.

After dinner, there's lots of singing and dancing. Then my
uncles raise me in my chair, and everyone dances around me.
It's part of bat mitzvah tradition.

I laugh, because it feels like I'll fall out of my chair! Everyone
is having fun, and so am I.

"Time for gifts!" my mother calls.

This is secretly a favorite part of mine too. It's better than
my birthday.

Before Hannah's bat mitzvah, she had to do a
mitzvah project. Can you think of other ways
people give back? How do other religions
support their communities? Why is this such
an important part of many religions?

SACRED TEXTS

Judaism has a 24-book sacred text called the Tanakh. The first 5 books are referenced most, called the Torah.

The Torah tells the story of how God created the world. It also talks about how Judaism and Jewish law developed.

The Nevi'im is the second section of the Tanakh. Its 8 books feature the writings of Hebrew prophets.

The third section of the Tanakh is the 11-book Ketuvim. It features poetry, philosophy, and history.

I receive a few books, a prayer shawl called a tallit, and a necklace. I also get a notebook for my writings. I get money for college too.

Did you know? During the bat or bar mitzvah party, many dance the "hora." This consists of the celebrant being lifted in a chair while others dance around.

Did you know? It is tradition to throw candy at the celebrant during the bat or bar mitzvah service!

Then it's back to celebrating. My cousin Amir asks me, "How was it to read in front of everyone?"

I laugh. "Terrifying." But then I see the look on his face. "But not bad."

He nods. "The party is worth it," he adds.

It is great to have my whole family together like this. Then I pause and tap Amir's shoulder. "Tag, you're it."

I run away. I may be grown up now that I've had my bat mitzvah. But I'm not too old for a game of tag!

ACTIVITY

MAKING LATKES

Latkes are a traditional Jewish food. They are often served during holidays. Here is how you can make your own.

INGREDIENTS:

5 large potatoes

1 onion

2 eggs

3 tablespoons (45 milliliters) of flour

Salt and pepper to taste

1 cup (237 mL) of canola oil

DIRECTIONS:

1. Peel the potatoes and chop into small pieces.

2. Finely chop the onions.

3. Mix the potatoes and onions together in a bowl.

4. In a dishtowel, squeeze liquid from the potato and onion mixture.

5. Beat the eggs in another bowl and add flour, salt, and pepper.

6. Add potato and onion mixture.

7. Heat 1 inch (2.5 centimeters) of oil in a pan. Add 6 tablespoons (90 mL) of the mix to the oil, flattening the cake with a spatula.

8. Cook for 4 minutes on each side.

Latkes can be served with different toppings, such as sour cream or applesauce, to add variety.

TIMELINE of MAJOR EVENTS

Circa 2000 BCE: Abraham moves his people to Canaan

Circa 1000 BCE: King David calls Jerusalem the capital of Judah

Circa 70 CE: Rabbis in Palestine begin creating the Tanakh

1492: Spain expels Jews

1840–1850: German Jews arrive in the United States, establishing Reform Judaism

1933: Adolf Hitler of the Nazi Party is named chancellor of Germany; promoting **anti-Semitism**, which is hostility against Jews

1939: World War II begins

1945: Holocaust and WWII end

1948: Israel is established as a state, creating a new home country for Jews

1967: Six-Day War is fought between Israel and Arab neighboring countries

2009: Rabbi Julie Schonfeld becomes the first female president of the Rabbinical Assembly, a Conservative movement rabbi organization

LEARN MORE

FURTHER READING

Marsico, Katie. *Judaism*. Ann Arbor, MI: Cherry Lake Publishing, 2017.

Rosinsky, Natalie M. *Judaism*. Mankato, MN: Compass Point Books, 2010.

Self, David. *The Lion Encyclopedia of World Religions*. Oxford, UK: Lion Children's, 2008.

WEBSITES

BBC Bitesize—What is Judaism?
https://www.bbc.co.uk/bitesize/topics/znwhfg8/articles/zh77vk7

Britannica Kids—Judaism
https://kids.britannica.com/kids/article/Judaism/353327

GLOSSARY

aliyah (ah-LEE-yah) being called up to read in a synagogue

anti-Semitism (an-tee-SEH-muh-tih-zuhm) hostility against Jews

bat/bar mitzvah (BAT/BAR MITZ-vuh) a Jewish coming-of-age ceremony for girls/boys

diaspora (dye-AAH-spuh-ruh) the relocation of Jews around the world due to conflict

famine (FAH-muhn) a food shortage, or hunger

Haftarah (haf-TOHR-uh) a portion of the Torah

icon (EYE-kahn) an important figure

kosher (KOH-shuhr) refers to food permitted for Jews by religious texts

latkes (LAHT-kuhz) pancakes made from grated potatoes

monotheism (mah-nuh-THEE-ih-zuhm) the belief in one God

plagues (PLAYGZ) diseases that spread quickly

polytheism (PAH-lee-thee-ih-zuhm) the belief in multiple gods

rabbi (RAH-bye) a Jewish religious leader

Shabbat (shuh-BAHT) the time between sundown Friday to sundown Saturday when Jews pray and reflect

s'udat mitzvah (soo-DAT MITZ-vah) the meal after a bat/bar mitzvah ceremony

synagogue (SIH-nuh-gohg) the temple for Jews

INDEX